How to Love Your Spouse's Lover
A Story of Forgiveness

Maurice Brailsford

Published By

BluSoul Worldwide Entertainment Group, Inc.

*MOVING FROM THE LAND OF BITTERNESS AND STRIFE
TO THE LAND OF HEALING AND PEACE*

ISBN 978-0-98-290310-0
How to Love Your Spouse's Lover

Scripture Quotations are taken from the King James Version of the Bible and are put into modern-day context and application.

Names, characters, places, and incidents are based on the author's own personal experience therefore names of persons and entities remain unnamed to protect the integrity of the story and the privacy of those involved. Any group or organization listed is for informational purposes only and does not imply endorsement or support of their activities or organization.

The author makes no apology for how the very **REAL** presence of God in this work of non-fiction may impact the reader's spiritual life. For ordering, booking, permission, or questions, contact the author.

Printed in the United States of America
SE 2012

Edited by: Shantae A. Charles for GOD Ideas, LLC
Cover Design: Marcia Nurse, Warrior Design, warriordesign.net
Design Management: Robert O. Charles, ROC Studios International, Inc.

How to Love Your Spouse's Lover
A Story of Forgiveness

Maurice Brailsford

How to Love Your Spouse's Lover
A Story of Forgiveness

Maurice Brailsford

Published By

BluSoul Worldwide Entertainment Group, Inc.
North Carolina

*MOVING FROM THE LAND OF BITTERNESS AND STRIFE
TO THE LAND OF HEALING AND PEACE*

Special Thanks

To my lovely wife Lisa McClendon-Brailsford, my ten wonderful children, wonderful parents, siblings and extended family. Without you, this testimony would not be possible.

How to Love Your Spouse's Lover
A Story of Forgiveness

Maurice Brailsford

TABLE OF CONTENTS

Forward

When I first heard the title of this book, I did a double take. I could not *believe* what my ears were hearing. There are so many undiagnosed illnesses that you can't help think that somehow people have brought some of these sicknesses upon themselves simply because of unforgiveness. This book will take you on a journey of love, resentment, and the triumphs of forgiveness. You will be challenged to examine your own life and be honest with yourself on whether or not you are truly walking in forgiveness.

Lisa McClendon-Brailsford

International Recording Artist

Reflection

Speechless; as an author, editor, teacher, and minister, words hardly ever fail me. But after reading the page-turning account of Maurice's life, I am truly humbled to have been given this opportunity to reflect.

From all appearances, Maurice strikes you as a respectful man who is formidable in anything he undertakes. What his outer-man does not convey is that he is a man who has been broken and then made whole through the power of God's forgiveness. As I read, I felt the heart and care of the Father for those imprisoned by unforgiveness.

Maurice's story is refreshing; it is not about blame or tearing others down; it's about honest feelings, it's about building broken lives, mending broken hearts and seeing others healed from their soul's diseases. Maurice is a modern-day Hosea with a right now Word for an adulterous generation. I pray that forgiveness unfolds and unfurls in you as you read this compelling testimony that resonates with love, faith, hope, forgiveness, and ultimately triumph through Christ.

Shantae A. Charles

Editor-In-Chief

Author's Forward

The story you're about to read is a true story of a man's love, loyalty, passion, betrayal and triumph in forgiveness. This is a story about my life as a young man who made the decision to choose between two lovers, his high school sweetheart and his promising football career. I was a football phenomenon and teenage father who gave up my dreams to go to college and play football to wed the mother of my unborn child. Torn between two lovers and feeling confused, I gave up those dreams to keep my family together. Through an unexpected turn of events, I went from being a man on top of the world to nearly destroying my entire life through seeking self-gratifying revenge. My younger brother reminded me that I had the opportunity to kill, or be killed, leaving my kids behind with the possibility of facing jail time or death, or I could become a legend and forgive what most would declare as unforgivable behavior. This compelling testimony is a story for all nationalities, races, and genders, young and old. It is about the ultimate power of forgiveness when faced with unimaginable and unexpected circumstances. My prayer is that you will be able to take the life lessons and move forward or help others move forward on their path to wholeness and healing.

Maurice Brailsford

Introduction

This is a story about how I chose to listen to the voice of the Lord and forgive my ex-wife the woman whom I loved and cherished for eighteen years, my junior high sweetheart, the woman I shared every dream and intimate moment with and her lover. I was moments away from the possibility of being put in jail or six feet under. I realize that I could not have made it without the love of God and the supernatural power of forgiveness.

This book reveals through my testimony and studies of the Word some basic principles and insights that I haven't heard taught anywhere else. Never before in the history of our country has there been such an on slaught of violent and hateful crimes committed in our society. Many newspapers, magazines, radio and television programs talk about the unprecedented murder rate, the unexplainable rage in our children, and hatred being dealt with in our homes and work places.

The multibillion dollar film industry has found these headliners to be sure box office hits year after year. We promote vicious violence and pay top dollar to see it but yet there's a constant wonder about why our youth are out of control. I've encountered so many people who have gone through the same thing I have experienced. Unfortunately the end of their story is behind bars, some of whom will never see freedom again. This book is about the ultimate truth of forgiveness. I am confident this book will bless you and possibly keep you from making some of the same foolish mistakes others have made in life. People are locked up because they chose not to forgive.

There are millions of people no longer with us today because someone took matters into their own hands and did not give their victim a chance to plead their case. People have been killed, beaten, tortured, spit on, lied on, and called racial slurs because they couldn't find it in their hearts to forgive. Wars have overtaken our cities right here in the United States of America because someone chose not to forgive or release someone from their debts.

Children are being raised in families where Mothers hate Fathers and unforgiveness stands like a wall between them. Some children suffer the rest of their lives because they look so much like their fathers. The threat and promise of divorce is at an alarming high, even in the church, which is responsible for teaching on love and forgiveness. Is anyone listening anymore? There are adult men and women that hate their mother or father because they grew up lonely or were raised by grandparents who were too elderly to spend quality time with them. The seeds of bitterness that were planted in childhood are now full grown trees of unforgiveness.

During a visit to a local prison, more than half of the men I met said they would kill their fathers if they ever met him. These men were angry that their fathers were not there for them while growing up. I have spoken to children who say they could never forgive their mother for choosing crack over them. Battered women shelters are filled with women who have been abused at the hands of an out of control, unforgiving man or partner. Some of the most vicious crimes in our society have occurred by someone unable to let go of what happened in their past. Take a brief look at your local news and you will quickly discover a society filled with intense rage and crimes because of unforgiveness. Instead of working to rectify these societal ills, many see these circumstances as a chance to capitalize on the pain of others.

My life is sweet now that I have forgiven my ex-wife and her lover. I can't tell you that it was easy. I know that it's no one but God who has wiped my mind clean of all of the hurt and the pain that I once walked in. I have married the love of my life and have been gifted with two more wonderful children in the process. I am now a Youth Director at my present church in the state of North Carolina and have traveled the world ministering to thousands of people about my past experiences. I am now working on the screen play to this book that will make you laugh, cry and prayerfully find freedom through forgiveness. I am now a Life Coach, motivational speaker, minister and promoter. I couldn't have orchestrated the direction that my life has taken even if I had tried to. My ex-wife and her lover have had dinner with us a time or two. I can actually say that I love them with the love of God. I pray for them day and night that God our Father would give them the wisdom to follow His direction. It is amazing what our Father is doing right now in our lives because of forgiveness.

Ancestry

On September 21, 1974, on a late Saturday night I became the firstborn son to teenage parents. My grandparents never encouraged abortion even though they thought their daughter was far too young to be a mother. My father on the other hand, was raised by a family of women, and had never had his father in his life. He would soon be faced with the challenges of marriage and raising a son. As a child, I remember my dad telling me about his first time meeting his father. While playing outside near his home, he was approached by a man driving a brand-spanking new Cadillac Deville.

> *"Are you James?" The mystery man asked.*
> *"Yes." My father replied.*
> *"I'm your father," the man said.*

At that moment, my Dad knew he never wanted his son to be affected by an absentee father. My father chose to forego his opportunities to go to college and play football because he didn't want to be absent from my life. Looking back, I realize how blessed my mother truly was. During the 1970's, a lot of women were being mistreated by men; either it was the drugs that were heavily influencing the culture then or the sexual revolution of free love and the opportunity to have multiple partners by practicing 'safe sex", a term that was new to the times. The popular lyrics, "Poppa was a rolling stone; wherever he laid his hat was his home," was reality for many and it left a lot of children disappointed and fatherless.

My father was raised in a single family home with his sister. He had an older brother that was in the service that he would get a chance to see every once in a while when he was home from the Vietnam War. His mother worked as a house keeper while trying to hold down the fort at home. My Dad's mother was abandoned while she was pregnant with my father. I know that it hurt my father because many times during our upbringing he would drive home the point to us that he didn't have a Father in his life. Those words became ingrained in our memory and helped us appreciate him more for being in our lives.

My father grew up defending himself. He didn't have anyone to teach him how to be a responsible man. With no father-figure of his own, he would look for love amongst the older kids in the neighborhood. He shared with me how it felt to look into the stands when he played football and not see anyone from his home cheering him on. His mom didn't have the time to watch him play either; she was too busy working to put food on the table. According to statistics, my dad was supposed to become an absentee, deadbeat father because he didn't have a Father in the home.

He explained to me that he would see his mother crying at times and didn't fully comprehend all of the sacrifices she was making. She would deny herself even the simple things just to see that her children were provided for. He recalled his mother having one or two dresses she would repeatedly patch so that she would have something to wear to work. He recalled that she didn't have a decent outfit to wear to church but she would send them to church so that they would have a foundation in God, as she did.

My father loved football as well; he wanted to play in the NFL one day and he excelled in it. He tried with all of his might not to become a neighborhood statistic. Everything would change once he met my mother and I was soon to follow. My father would learn how to work on cars and balance a check book from his sister's husband. He always sought help on how to be a great husband and father.

My mother grew up the exact opposite; she had her mother and father in the home. I heard a lot of stories about how my grandfather was a rolling stone and how my grandmother went through a lot with him in their younger days but, hey they never said that their marriage would be perfect either. My mother, however, was raised in the church and surrounded by church goers. Even as a little girl she always wanted to have God in her life. I was told that when she was about four or five years old, every time someone would ask her how she was doing she would say, "Fine, thanks the Lord."

My mother was raised to ask for what she wanted and my grandmother would make sure that it happened. When my mother was younger, my grandmother would ask each of the children what they wanted for breakfast, lunch or dinner. My grandmother would cook each one her children a personal breakfast. In these uncertain economic times, most parents would balk at this request.

The first time my mother met my father she was fourteen and he was fifteen years old. She was not able to have company from a boy but he did say she could only take company from one person. My dad had hit the jackpot; he was favored to get by the restrictions. My mom said my father had this huge afro and she said it was longer than hers. My grandmother thought that he was a teenage girl.

My father was able to glean from my grandfather what it meant to be a man in a home raising a family. Within a year my mother was pregnant with me. My father had to make a decision that would change his life forever. He made a decision to stick it out, become a father and not go off to college. My upbringing would play a profound part of how I would handle my own life challenges.

Childhood

My parent's close-knit family grew to include two additional sons and one daughter. My family was always filled with laughter, music, funny stories and childish pranks. The picture perfect marriage was distorted the day my father brought home a little girl-- his daughter from another woman. I quickly took on my mother's side in the matter, feeling hurt and betrayed yet unable to voice my mother's sentiments.

I grew up just like any other child: mischievous at times, selfish, and wanting things to be done my way a majority of the time. At the age of nine, I fell in love for the first time; football became the love of my life. I wanted to live out my father's dream of becoming a professional football player. At a young age, my father made sure that I was in every football camp and every year I played on a Pop Warner football team. Football was not just another sport to me; it was like an adolescent boy who had been awestruck by a beautiful young adolescent girl for the first time: The high rush of adrenaline, sweaty palms, the anticipation of the unknown, the challenge of beast versus beast. I ate, slept, and dreamt football. I was determined that I would stop at nothing to play in the pros, or so I thought.

By Junior High, in the late eighties, when ninth grade was the top of the class, I was still playing football and I took it very seriously. I had recently become a hero during our championship game, and though it was an incredible experience, what happened my ninth grade year would change my life forever. One day, while on my way to fifth period class, I heard this airy, intriguing voice from behind me asking, "Hey, boy, are you bow-legged?" I turned around, and--BAM! Standing before me was this beautiful young girl with long black silky hair, piercing eyes and the most beautiful skin. I replied sarcastically, trying not to show how awestruck I was, "I don't know; am I?" She smiled as she walked away.

That brief encounter left me mesmerized. Before then, I had never looked at girls in such a way. I didn't recall any previous desires to have a girlfriend. After all, I was still dating football. Later that day, on my way home, I remember saying, "That will be my wife one day," I had several dreams about her being my wife. I didn't quite know how to react to my feelings. My parents had never really talked to me about sex.

My first introduction to sex was through pornography that I watched with my older cousins in secret. I was so wet behind the ears that I actually thought the pathway to a woman's intimate garden was through her navel! This girl had shaken me to my core and I had never felt that way before: My heart was pounding, and all of a sudden, my appearance and the way I carried myself became very important to me. I no longer wanted to be the football tough guy; I had found another love. I was now faced with the challenge of choosing to love one or the other-but did I have to?

Over the next few days, we would have hit and miss conversations. I couldn't believe that something else had been able to capture my attention besides football. I had it all figured out; I had concluded that with her being a year younger than I, that, *surely her parents were not going to allow her to come to my house or anywhere else*, so I would still be able to put my all into football. One day while my friends and I were hanging out at my locker talking football, she approached me and asked, "Hey, boy, you want to be my boyfriend; yes or no?" I covertly spelled out Y-E-S because I didn't want my boys to think I was going soft on them.

I never thought that girl in the hallway could ever take my focus off of something that I had grown to love and worship for years. I was within years of trying out for the NFL, within reach of walking across that NFL podium on draft day as my parents and siblings all watched my name being called to join a NFL team. Maybe I wouldn't have to choose after all.

I can tell you the truth, that for me, it was love at first sight and to this day, I can't explain everything that was going through my mind. There are a lot of people that have goals and dreams but then something else comes between that and it seems like you can never get excited about what meant the world to you from the beginning. We had a wonderful summer just talking and laughing about how much we were meant for each other. She wasn't allowed to date or go out with anyone and now that I look back on it, her parents did the right thing. I told my daughters that they weren't allowed to date until they got married (I guess you can figure that one out). At the time I thought that her parents were mean, but in the end, I appreciate everything they did for my ex-wife because they didn't let her run wild like a lot of the other girls at my school were doing.

That summer was the best summer of my life because I started thinking about what it would be like to go to college and have my girlfriend come up and visit during her summer breaks. I started to let my mind go into places that it shouldn't have, especially at that age. I was envisioning my future through rose colored glasses. I saw us buying that pink house that she always talked about with the kitchen on the top floor and the huge yard with a couple of dogs with lots of children.

I didn't think that I could be happier with anyone or anything else. If my life were a movie script, this would have been the best young love story ever. The only way we could talk on the phone was when her parents went to the store or were away from home and she would call me to see how I was doing. It was a funny relationship, but I wasn't complaining at all because I didn't have to give up football. I could kick it with my girl and keep my game.

Becoming a Man

My transition into senior high school would be the test of our relationship. Over the summer I grew a couple of inches; I was no longer that skinny kid looking for direction. I had become a young man with facial hair and my now- muscular physique had become the main attraction for all the freshmen, junior and senior girls. I thought I was all that and a bag of chips because the girls in the high school gave me compliments every day. There were even some senior girls that wanted my phone number and followed me to class.

My grueling high school schedule made it difficult for my girlfriend and I to talk as much as we had been used to in the past. Her parents were very strict and did not allow her to take phone calls or go out by herself. It began to put some strain on our relationship and I began to test the waters by dating other people, but it was never quite the same. Although the other girls were able to go out and attend my football games, I wasn't happy. I was confident that my girlfriend was at home watching my football highlights on the evening news.

During my senior year, I had become one of the top athletes in my high school. Colleges had started pursuing me and I was excited about the opportunity to visit and attend college. The thought of leaving her for college didn't seem right. I had recently experienced leaving her behind in junior high to make my transition into senior high, and I did not like that feeling. My attitude towards football began to change noticeably. I fell more in love with her and became less interested in football. My fantasies of her became more frequent and eventually I would have the opportunity to live out those fantasies.

One day while I daydreamed of my girlfriend and us being able to be together without anyone telling us what to do, the devil began to bring lustful thoughts into my mind and I couldn't shake it. I knew that if I allowed the enemy to get me off track with vain imaginations, it could possibly take my future and destroy my dreams, but I had no active Word in me because my mother and father didn't press us about going to church anymore. I didn't fully understand that everything that I had dreamt of and had worked hard to accomplish and succeed in was flying out the window.

Being a virgin, I began to prepare myself to engage in sexual activity with the love of my life. It was something that I thought I was ready for, I had no experience; I had no one to tell me that this could cause a lifetime of drama, hurt, despair, and confusion (I wasn't exactly seeking counsel, either). My only frame of reference was what I gleaned from movies be it pornographic or romantic comedies. I thought that it was time to „sow my wild oats" because I was a senior in high school and everyone was doing it.

I remembered my uncle telling me that girls "Stank", but when I tested the fields for the first time I knew that he was only trying to scare me into compliance. I didn't know that the „spreading of my oats" would cause a little one in my image to be manifested. I had a choice and a chance to say no but I didn't. I thought that we had a match made in heaven that nothing would ever come between us. It was my birthday, September 21, 1991, and that was the day that my fantasies became a reality. That was the day that I would learn that there was in fact another pathway into a woman's intimate garden and it was *not* through her navel.

So, I blew it; I had sex with my girlfriend for the first time! All of the home training and warnings I had received had gone unrecognized as I decided to take my relationship to the next level. I would have never guessed that my one night of pleasure would result in an eighteen-year parental responsibility (Truth be told, I will always be a parent, but I won't always be their guardian).

I am telling you now, teenagers, as well as adults: it only takes one time and you can find yourself having responsibilities that will call you Mommy or Daddy for the rest of your life. Research now proves that the parts of your brain that handle rational thinking are still being formed and developed through your teenage years. This may have played a part in my eagerness to throw caution to the wind.

My girlfriend began to change and her emotions seemed to be all over the place; I didn't know what was going on. One of the first emotions that teens experience after engaging in premarital sex is depression. A month after we had sex she told me that she had bought a pregnancy test from the store and that she was pregnant.

I couldn't believe it. I was shocked and afraid I didn't know what to say. I only could imagine what her parents and my parents were going to say. I finally calmed down after a couple of weeks and I started trying to plan our life and see how we were going to work everything out. I knew those nine months were going to be crazy.

I didn't want to tell my Mom. All of those years she had prayed so hard, binding and loosing, rebuking the devil so that we wouldn't make the same mistake that her and my dad had made years ago. I hated to tell her that I made my own choice to have sex without being married and especially without using a condom.

I could picture her face as she wondered why God had let her down because he did not answer her prayer about her children not having babies out of wedlock. I knew my mom was going to be in tears because she had prayed over us every day and I felt bad because I knew that God had nothing to do with my mistake-- it was my choice. I was terrified but at the same time, I felt that I had to become a man quickly. Being in high school, playing ball and having your first child were a lot on a sixteen year old boy's plate.

The only thing I could do was think positive so I started to imagine my future wife and the baby being at my football games and sitting in the crowds cheering for me. What I didn't imagine was how expensive a baby and a wife would be. I began to turn what at that time was a negative into a positive, and that's what helped me get through school that year. I remember my girlfriend picking up weight, her ninety-pound frame filling out with motherly curves. She would let me feel the baby move in her stomach and that made me really nervous.

Months after learning we would be teenage parents, things started to take a drastic turn. My girlfriend and mother of my unborn child became very paranoid and controlling; she didn't want me to leave her and go away to college. I finally got up the nerve to tell her that I wanted my life back and I told her I wasn't feeling the whole thing about being with her because she was having my baby because I felt like she was trying to control me. The news made her even more paranoid and enraged. She threatened to tell my parents she was pregnant if I broke it off with her. Her threat was soon fulfilled and our parents were devastated by the news.

I felt like I had let everyone down; my parents had such high hopes and dreams for my life. They had wanted so much for me not to go down that same path they had trod some seventeen years earlier. College had been the path that everyone was counting on me to take; football was the hope for my future. My parents were really hurt because they did their best to keep me from travelling down the same path that they did. Surprisingly though, my parents soon got over it and life went on. Thankfully, they didn't hold a grudge, even though I knew in my heart that my dad had to be sick to his heart that his oldest son that he had invested all of this time in was not going to pursue the goals he had dreamed about all of his life.

My mom called my girlfriend's parents and boy that encounter went no better; her parents had wanted the same for her. My father had always been there for me and I said to myself growing up that I never wanted to have babies without being there for them. I remember telling the Lord to take the taste of playing football away from me so I could do the right thing and if he saw down the line where I could play, then blesses me on down the line.

One of the saddest days of my life was the day I announced to my coaches, family and friends that was going to step up and take care of my responsibility as a father, foregoing my opportunity to attend college and play football. Many people thought that I had lost my mind including my coaches and peers. I really couldn't see straight; I wanted to be like my father who had stayed with my mom after finding out that she was pregnant. I wanted the same life for my son. I just couldn't leave. I wanted to beat the odds and make it work. I wanted to prove so many people wrong and show them that I was a winner, a champion and not a quitter. But a relationship that is formed out of sin or a life that is lived in sin sometimes hand us cards that we cannot play.

Teen Husband and Father

On February 7, 1992, I wed that beautiful young girl with that intriguing voice, silky black hair, piercing eyes and the most beautiful skin. Suddenly I was no longer just a seventeen year old high school football hero; I was also a young father and husband. Yes, I did it. I made the decision to not have two lovers and much to everyone's surprise, for the first time, football had taken the backseat on this long journey.

As for my teen bride, I worshipped the ground she walked on; she was my pride and prize. There was never any doubt in my mind that she would ever betray me. After all, I had sacrificed a lot of things to prove my love for her. I gave up my passion, football, something I had loved for many years. I'd given up the chance to go to college. Now, as a new husband and father with no life experience, we moved in with my parents. It was very clear that her mother wanted nothing to do with me or our marriage.

My mother, without any hesitation, had escorted us downtown to get married. After all, it was the right thing to do, right? Time passed by like a storm cloud; my wife's belly looked as though it was ready to burst at any moment. She began to have labor pains and her stomach became harder and harder. I had to take her to the hospital and boy was I glad to see the doctor.

June 22, 1992, came quicker than I thought; the big day was finally here. I was content, overjoyed, happy, nervous, scared all at the same time. She was in labor for a very long time. *The baby is not coming soon enough,* I thought, pacing the floor back and forth for hours. The doctor told us that because it was my wife's first child that his head was too big and that they would have to use utensils to try to get him out. As a teen mother, her body was not yet fully mature to handle the adult responsibility of bearing a child. I prayed and hoped that all would be well.

My first child was a son; his name, in the English origin, means high-spirited or sword. The Irish meaning is prince or brave and I see that in him now. *Wow! I'm having my first child this is so crazy,* I thought, because I found myself in the same situation that my father was in over sixteen years ago. *My firstborn son is here; he is so precious to me and looks just like his mom with his long silky black hair coco cream skin, ready to live in the world.* I kissed him constantly over and over because I saw myself in him. He smelled like roses and berries his skin was so smooth. I watched the little guy move around and open his eyes for the first time. I am wondered what he was thinking and I made a commitment to myself that I was going to be the best father I could be for him.

I didn't know how anyone could hurt someone so precious. I didn't want to leave his side. God is awesome! Having a son; that just does something to a man. I had to find a J-O-B and soon I would find a nice job working at an alarm company. I was the youngest person to ever work at this company. I was getting paid making some money while staying with my parents. I was on top of the world and thought all was well.

My perfect little family world took a major turn the day I learned that my wife had been to Georgia and had been with her childhood sweetheart. She told me that all she did was kiss him. This guy grew up with her in Georgia and she would see him on her visits with her brother and his father. I wanted to believe the best but I had already begun to see the signs of trouble. My beautiful bride had once again become very possessive. I felt trapped; it was like revisiting high school all over again.

Her leisure trip to Georgia had afforded her the opportunity to reconnect with a love from the past. I would learn of this betrayal through a letter she had to written me; that was the final straw. We were in strife, bitterness and everything else you could imagine. The toll of being married so young and being parents was too much of a strain for such a young couple. We were arguing every day and I was really missing football. This was my chance to break free and break free is exactly what I did.

That long buried desire to play football continued to linger. I began to see my high school teammates playing college football on television and I was faced with constant pressure from family members to return to school. Finally my mother took me to a local college up the road from where I lived. I applied and I got accepted. I had taken my college entrance test and passed it, so I could play football again.

As I trained I found out that I still possessed the same talent that allowed me to play as if I had never left the game. Things were looking up; I had my freedom and my family back home was with my parents. In spite of the possessive and controlling behaviors that continued to arise, somehow this young lady still somehow managed to hold my heart.

The day before I left for college, my wife told me she was pregnant. Now, to be honest, when I found out that she was having another child, I felt it came at the wrong point in our marriage. I was trying to make this football team and the way the head coach encouraged me, led me to believe I had a great chance to make it. Three months went by and I could no longer stay focused on football and try to work to send money back home. I left college to become gainfully employed.

My wife and I moved into a two-bedroom apartment and God blessed us to get furniture through the help of some family members. I remember saying this was no way to bring a child into the earth. I was having a baby girl and it was different from having a son because in my mind having a girl made me softer and helped me to understand the reason why I was still here on earth. I didn't want to let my daughter down. I didn't want her to come to this world not being able to look up to the man that helped give her life.

June 21, 1993 came too quick. I remember running six miles from my apartment to the hospital to see the birth of my daughter. My wife's mom was still upset with me for getting her daughter pregnant in the first place so when she came to pick her up to take her to the hospital she wouldn't let me ride with them. I was thinking about my life all the way to the hospital, thinking about all the times that I had dreamed about playing football and walking across that stage in New York and being drafted by the Dallas Cowboys and now look at me-- eighteen years old with a son and now a daughter on the way, my dreams crushed.

I pushed those thoughts aside and I began to thank God for a healthy child and that nothing would happen to my wife while she was delivering. It was funny how it happened that the Bulls were playing the Phoenix Suns and John Paxson had just hit the winning shot and when my wife held her hands up to cheer her water broke; now that was a way to bring a child into the world! When I got to the hospital drenched with sweat, tired from the run, I went into the room where my wife lay; her expression seemed to ask, *what we do from here.* I had thought several times about going into the military even though I was scared because of the war and the thought of leaving my family never to return.

When my wife delivered my baby girl, I remembered saying that this was one of the prettiest babies I had ever seen. She was very bright with beautiful skin and she looked just like me and my wife combined and she reminded me of a little princess. I felt that I was on top of the world that and I had to make a better life for my family. I vowed at that time that I would not allow our arguing to cause us to separate.

Our firstborn daughter's name meant pure, wise child, full of joy or beloved. Having her really brought peace in my life; she represented the best of what I wanted life to be. I held her all night and I even asked the doctors if I could stay overnight in the room with my wife and the baby. I sang songs to her all night as she lay across my chest as if I were the only thing in the world that mattered to her. My daughter was my pride and joy and I realized that I needed her in my life. She was my flower, my princess and precious jewel. I remember saying that I was going to seek God first and all of his righteousness because I didn't want to be on welfare and food stamps for the rest of my life.

My father raised me better than that and taught me through his life to be a provider for the family. I was ready for a change so I enlisted in the military. Out of everything I had undertaken, I felt like this was the right move. Once again I had to make a decision; love or football. I enrolled in the military to serve my country and provide for my wife and two children. I loved my wife; I really wanted to make it work especially after the infidelity that she committed prior to me leaving for college. I had made mistakes as well; at eighteen years old, I was nowhere near perfect.

I knew that my Father had been unfaithful to my mom and they had worked through the incident; their marriage had turned out well so I felt I could forgive her for the transgression that she had done against me. My mother was a real role model; she always taught us that to the pure all things are pure. She knew that it would be tough but her motto was you could make it through anything; just put your trust in the Lord and he will see you through. I never wanted things to be easy; I always wanted to be a hero in any way, to come out on top regardless.

I just felt like if we made it, then I would be able to prove the people wrong. Well, after going in the military, I found out that I was going to be deployed to Japan. This would be a real test for me because I had never been away from home before like this. I was a stranger in a foreign land. After the death of my collegiate friends, I decided to give my life to the Lord. I wanted to be real with myself and my family. I realized that if I wanted to make my relationship with my wife better and wanted to be a role model to my children, I needed to put my life in the Lord's hands.

Overseas

Okinawa, Japan was a season of refreshing in my life. I had made peace with my God. I began to mature spiritually. I once again found my way back to football, playing in the Military League. I had again become a hero of the game, so I thought. I was known throughout the Military Bases. I had become an instant celebrity to them. I would stop at the red light and people would literally get out of their cars and take pictures of me. I noticed they really loved American people.

October 24, 1996, my wife gave birth to our third child, my second daughter. This was tough because in Okinawa, Japan we were far away from home and going through some terrible trials in our relationship. I had turned my life over to Christ at this time and was really on fire for the Lord. My wife on the other hand was really not feeling our relationship.

I remember nights being alone and wondering, *how long will I go through this drama*? It was like the love in my wife's heart for me had disintegrated. I remember her taking a test one day saying that she was pregnant; I really didn't know how to react. We had no connection, and it was like I was staying with a woman that didn't want to touch me. I could do nothing right in her eyes. My house was filled with hate, bitterness and strife. My wife had started to think that maybe we had gotten married too young and that, maybe, I wasn't the man for her.

She began to be influenced by a different group of friends and they were telling her that she was too young to be married and she needed to get out and live a little. It was like no one saw that we had a family with three children. It was as though they wanted to drive her away from her destiny. I had heard that the island of Japan where we were stationed was full of evil spirits and that most of the marriages ended in divorce. The Island was overrun with the spirit of fornication and the spirit of lust and if you got caught up in it and stopped really seeking the Lord's face, you too could become a casualty.

With everything that was going on, news of her pregnancy took me by surprise. I had my doubts due to her being out in the street and not being in places that she said she was going to. I prayed and asked the Lord to work things out between us so that this little one would come into a loving environment instead of hate, and the Lord answered my prayers. God moved some of those ungodly influences off the island; either it was their time to leave or they would lose interest in being friends with my wife.

My second daughter's name means "wise". This must have been God's doing because I think if this child hadn't come, we would have divorced then. There was such a stronghold on my wife's life that I prayed for her every day for a year, thanking God for changing her life and causing her to love me the way a wife was supposed to love a husband. This daughter brought a lot of joy to my life. She was very beautiful with lots of hair and she seemed smarter than the average baby because she would talk and make noises as if she was listening to every word I said. She loved to dance and smile. She gave us relief as well because we were able to realize that God put her in our lives to keep us together. Things were indeed looking up. I began to see changes in the both of us. We became leaders in our church in Japan and I studied diligently under my pastor. Things were really great. All was calm...for the moment.

One night I received a call from a former roommate buddy. He began to tell me that he saw my wife's car at another officer's residence. My wife had a routine when she would leave the house; she would call home when she got were she was just to make sure that me and the kids were okay and then I wouldn't hear from her again until later in the night. She had me fooled because she was going to college there and she told me she was going to work on a class project with some of her classmates. After he told me this, I began to question where she was and then she began to get defensive. I guess you could say, after years of relationship ups and downs, I had become a bit wiser in how to approach the situation.

Every Thursday she would leave the house at a certain time. At my direction, a friend of mine began to follow her, and sure enough, he saw her pick up a young man, driving him to a Military department store. I was still a little naïve; I had to have more proof. I didn't want to believe it; I wanted to give her the benefit of the doubt.

I didn't have my family to talk to; they were all the way back in the States.

So, one day when she left the house, I took the house phone off the hook and headed out in a rage. I knew if she called she would think that I was on the phone because we didn't have call waiting. I had my friend to show me where the car was parked and what barracks she had gone into. I had determined that I was going to knock on every door if I had to. I had already confirmed that it was her car because I noticed our *wedding* ring in the cup holder! Now, it made sense why she couldn't stand to touch me. There was the possibility that there was another man involved; now I *had* to find her.

I had a neighbor watching the kids for me so I wasn't worried about them. I had been looking for my wife all night when suddenly, I heard a familiar tune in the distance. As it turned out I didn't have to knock on every door after all. Hurriedly, I moved toward the melody. It became apparent to me that the tune was so familiar because it was *my* mixed tape I had created for us! I balled up my fist and knocked on the door. The guy who answered the door, (who had borrowed the CD from my wife's boyfriend!) directed me one door over to find them.

I must have awakened the whole world as I banged on that steel door. As he opened the door, it was apparent that he had no idea who I was or what this whole situation was about. I wasted no time, announcing who I was, demanding to see my wife. Half-dressed and in complete shock, she ran for safety, not knowing what frame of mind I was in. I can't say that I knew what frame of mind I was in either. On his knees, begging for mercy for his life, the guy began to state his case, claiming that he didn't know she was married and to not hit him. I thought about putting his nose in his head and that would have killed him instantly.

There was another side to me as well that calmed me down and it was like all the rage that I had bottled up, waiting to explode, just...calmed. I had just heard a message on how Jesus forgave those that killed him and hung him on a cross. It was like the love of Christ in me forgave that young man right where he kneeled. I did one of the craziest things that a person could do having just caught his wife in adultery; I grabbed my wife and took her home.

After that incident, my wife apologized and asked me to forgive her. I did it without hesitation because I loved her and my children. I knew that I had to take my family back and I had to make sure that I prayed for my wife daily. I felt like she never had a childhood. I really felt in my heart that we had our children too young and it had never allowed her to mature as a young woman and enjoy life.

Thinking back, I felt like I was her scapegoat. That was the last time that we went through something like that overseas. My wife's heart changed towards me and we began to work on a „makeup baby". I felt pretty good because she had been faithful to me and was active in the church and helping me in ministry. I was happy because this is what I prayed for and the Lord had heard my prayers.

Return to the States

It was time to leave Japan; we had orders to go to California. My wife was excited because she had always wanted to move there. She loved the Hollywood look and she had always wanted to be a singer or actress. I was happy as well because my coach in the military had some hook up to one of the pro football teams in California. This was it; *I was going to make the pro league after all*, I thought. My wife surprised me when she said she was pregnant with baby number four! Yes, four! I was doing great, we loved each other like crazy, and those days of hate and strife were over.

I had been ministering on the streets of Japan with my local church and I had seen God do a lot for me and my family. I was into sports and really enjoying life. My wife went through a lot of complications with this fourth child in the womb. The doctors said she was too weak to carry any more babies. They said she had conceived too many children at a young age and that because of the way her uterus was tilted, it would be hard for her to have a baby. I was on my face every day praying to the Lord asking him to not allow anything bad to happen to any one of my children. God performed a miracle for us.

At one point we thought that my wife had miscarried but I just continued to pray, telling the doctors that my God would see this pregnancy through. They just thought that I was a young naïve kid who thought I knew it all and that I was going to be shocked the way life handed out its lessons, but in the end they were the ones that were shocked by the power that our God demonstrated. Despite the doctor's unfavorable prognosis, my wife went to full term and the baby came out fine.

Our fourth child and third daughter represented the peace of the Lord that was on our side, and was named to honor that. We moved to Monterey, California and that's where she was born. This was fun times because I was still seeking a pro football team to play for. Even though I was in the military, my dream was being able to suit up for a pro football team.

I had seen so much that the Lord had done for me and my family and my children. We were young, we had four little ones, and it looked like we had them coming one after the next, but God knew what he was doing and the babies just kept coming. Although I was proud of my family, I questioned our actions in continuing to keep having children. Feeling more and more pressure, I had to do something. I felt it was imperative to pursue this passion to play football. I went to several free agent combines for pro football players and finally the military released me.

We moved back to Jacksonville were I need to get some film of me in action to send to the pro football teams. I had an agent, and I was set to go. I had decided to play semi-pro. I loved the game so much that I wanted to do whatever I could to make it; even the smell of the grass energized me. I was back! I had made the cut! Playing in the semi-pros really made me believe that I could play in the pro football league. I did great in the semi-pro league; I was considered one of the best Linebackers in semi-pro and was asked to play in the all-star game in Tampa, Florida.

My agent was ecstatic; he called me after the all-star game and said that he had a job lined up for me up in Texas and he wanted me to come up there for a couple of months and work. He said that he could possibly help me land on an arena team that could possibly give me a shot to play in the pros. I asked myself, *is this really happening*? I had gotten the big break I needed. My excitement overwhelmed me. I was certain that my wife would be happy for me, for us, that she would see this as an awesome opportunity, but the sad look that she gave me confirmed the insecurities that lay within in her as she confessed that she was afraid that I would leave her with the kids. I tried to reassure her that I would never leave her and the kids. But the more I pleaded my case the more she was convinced that I should not go.

I called my agent and regretfully told him that I was not going to accept the offer to go to Texas. Everyone warned me that I was making a big mistake but I had decided that I was going to do all I could to keep my family together, just like my father did. The pain of walking away from yet another chance in the pros pierced through my soul like a sword, cutting deep. I had to find a job again and I was led to a desk job calling people about the debts that they owed my company.

Soon, we were at it again and when my wife told me that she was pregnant for the fifth time, I nearly cried because I knew that we could not afford another child at this point in our lives. I called a family member who encouraged me, telling me that, "If God allows you to have another child that means he will help you take care of it." That really hit my spirit and ministered to me because I knew that the Bible declared the womb was blessed and the man blessed who had his quiver full of children. So, I picked up my frown and began to praise God.

This son, when he came out, was big and strong and we wanted to name him after one of God's angels. Speaking of angels, my wife wanted to name him Angel but I wanted him to have a name that would stick. When our fifth child came home from the hospital he was very quiet. There was just something about him that made me excited, maybe it was because his hands and feet were huge and that meant to me he was going to be a football player (smile).

My mind set at this time was to do everything I could in order to keep my head above water. I was trying to land a good job to support my growing clan. My second son's personality was so quiet and calm, nothing seemed to bother him then and even now he is cool as the summer breeze. I worked even harder trying to put in overtime any chance I got. I remember praying and encouraging my co-workers and guiding them to church. I was just on fire for God; I knew that if I was going to go all out for a man that died for me over two thousand years ago, I wanted to go hard for God. People began to notice me and ask me for prayer every day. I was happy that I made the choice to let go of football and make a fresh start winning souls for God.

Finding Favor with God

God began to elevate us at our church we were attending in Jacksonville and people began to see the gifts and talents that God had equipped me with to evangelize. My wife and I were a part of a huge outreach ministry that the Lord had given to me while we were in Okinawa, Japan. As a young man, I was on fire for God and just didn't care what people said about me; I just wanted to fulfill the purpose of God for my life and bring my family with me.

One day my Pastor challenged me. He said that he had given this assignment to many people before me and no one had been able to accomplish it thus far. He said that if I brought fifty people to church, and if they all graduated from our eight-week New Member's course, that he would match my salary bringing me on full time to work in ministry. I was excited but I knew that I loved my church and I enjoyed bringing people to church anyway, so I said to myself *I love the challenge, but even if my pastor doesn't bring me on full time I wouldn't be upset.* I just kept up with the people that I was bringing to church and taking through the New Member's course.

The Lord was allowing people to come my way that didn't have a church home and were looking for a place to fellowship. God had anointed me for the task because it had never been that easy to witness to people and bring them to church. I remember getting to the fiftieth person within a year's time and saying to myself, *the Lord God is shining his favor on me from heaven.* When my Pastor found out, he wanted to meet with me and he congratulated me on a job well done. He said that he was going to bring me on board full time. I remember telling my Pastor that whenever the Lord was ready for me to come on full time that He was going to make a way and I left it at that.

The Lord at that time allowed my heart to be tested because he knew that I loved my church and my Pastors and he also knew that my dream and the desire of my heart was to become a full time Evangelist of the Gospel. I just wanted the timing to be right so when I came on full time, that would be the end of me ever working a secular job in my life. I loved my leadership not for what they could do for me, but who they were. I wanted to do something for them. I recognized that my destiny was tied into my leaders. My Pastors loved me for who I was and not what I looked like. Here I was, a man with crazy looking hair with a long beard. On the outside, I looked crazy but they saw the Jesus on the inside of me. That's why I would always serve my Pastors because when I was down and out they believed in me and they loved me in spite of what I looked like.

God is doing a new thing in church leadership and he is allowing them to see what's in the heart of men. Religious spirits are being rejected by the saints because all these vain traditions have done was separate the people of God. Pure religion according to the Bible is to take care of the widow and the fatherless, to feed the hungry, to visit the sick and those in prison; that's true religion. The devil couldn't stop the church, so he joined it and now he operates through man-made self-righteous deeds and religious restrictions that oppress believers.

Now you have a white church and a black church and all sorts of church denominations and creeds. Hey, Church, wake up! There are people dying while we are focused on who and what we don't like about each other. People are laughing at the Church and calling us hypocrites, self-righteous, pious critics and backstabbers. We were put here to be soul winners and lead people to Jesus. If we can rejoice in heaven together, then we should be able to rejoice on earth together. Now, go share that!

In 2003, my Pastors as well as the other leaders in the church saw what we were doing in the church and in the community and recommended us for ordination to be Evangelists for the church. This was a fun time in my life because of all the things that I went through and had accomplished due to my Lord and Savior Jesus Christ. I was finally seeing clear, I saw the purpose of the Lord for my life. I had been through a lot but nothing was going to stop me from fulfilling the vision and the dreams that the Lord had put in me.

I had a lot of people telling me how fired up I was about Jesus and how much of a blessing that I had been to them. I even had someone to tell me that I was fired up now but they wanted to see how fired up I was going to be in five years. Good or bad, I took that as a challenge because I knew the race wasn't given to the swift but to those that had endured to the end. Though it's not a Bible verse, the statement was still true. I didn't want to be a person that was only fired up for the Lord for a season; I wanted to be fired up for the Lord for a lifetime. I know a lot of people say that they don't care what others are saying about them but I really did care what others around me thought of me. Even Jesus, the Son of God wanted to know what others thought of him. I believe the people around you know you best and if they think that you are a jerk and you claim that you are not aware or even appear surprised, then, nine times out of the ten you might want to evaluate what they are saying; don't be afraid to take a good look at yourself.

Being recognized by my leadership was the most important thing for me because that let me know that they depended on me to be a part of the team that is fitted together in unity. The day my wife and I were ordained in front of the church and my family, it was one of the best moments of my life. My grandmother was there watching from the crowd and she was so happy for me, knowing everything that I went through. I knew that God had seen fit to put us in place to be a blessing to more people but that it came with more responsibilities.

The road looked long from a distance but God was always there and he continued to demonstrate his love for us. When the world says that we couldn't do it or it that it couldn't be done, the Lord would just show up and show out. I wouldn't have traded my life or my experiences for anything. I am happy that every trial and tribulation came to make me strong even when I felt like giving up at times and going my own way. I knew that this was the beginning of our prosperity and vision that God had for our lives.

I could remember being in my principal's office because I was in trouble for something I had done wrong and I would pray to God to give me another chance and that if He would get me out of this one I wouldn't do wrong again. The principal would come up to me and say, "I know that what you've done deserves a call to your father but I will give you another chance," and I would just cry out to the Lord and thank him for saving my rear end. I could not believe that a child that was saved from death, hell and jail would ever amount to anything. Throughout my life I would cry sometimes and want to be someone else, because at one point, I had gotten in a lot of trouble with my parents and my wife. Just to see God give me favor with men and women just surprised me and it made me thankful, loving the Lord that much more.

My wife and I were having our sixth child and things were looking bright for us. The only thing I thought about was, *how could* the Lord allow two young parents to have this many kids? *Wow, another baby on the way.* I was okay with this because I realized that with every child, we were blessed more and more. The babies were coming so fast that I was not able to keep up. This was comical for a man and woman to be so young with six children.

My wife wanted to name my third son after me but I wanted my son to have his own identity. Boy did he come out looking just like my brother when he was young. He was very long and thin but he had basketball hands. I was excited because the more boys you had the better chance you had to put a couple in college and if you were blessed enough you might be able to get one or two to go pro (smile). That was my dream and now I had that dream for my sons. My sixth child and third son was the trickster and even now he is always playing a joke on someone and getting into trouble, looking you in the face so innocently and lying like the devil. You have to watch him because he will get into trouble like nobody's business. I know out of all of my children he will be the one that outshines the rest; he has that 'Wow Factor" about him.

We were so happy even though we were in an apartment, but with baby number six, we *had* to get a bigger place. Our credit was not the best at this time and we didn't have anyone to co-sign for us. Someone in our apartments had noticed that my wife was pregnant and since we were on the third floor they took it upon themselves to inform the apartment manager. We were told that before she had the baby we had to be out of the apartment because we had too many people staying there. I knew that the Lord would take care of us so I began to thank him for His kindness and grace.

My wife was saddened by our situation and she had done a lot of searching for us to find another place to stay and there seemed to be nothing available. I had a cousin that called and ministered to me and he said that with every baby there comes an increase and that was enough to lift my spirits and shout to the Lord of glory to give Him the praise. The next week, my wife found some larger apartments that were right across the street from us and there was more than enough space to fit a family of eight. When the people checked our credit, it didn't show anything negative and they allowed us to move in without any problems.

The time for baby number six to enter the world had come and we had more than enough clothes, pampers and milk. God is so faithful to all of his children, especially the ones that love him and keep his commandments. This baby was like no other; he looked like a warrior that was ready to stump on the devils neck. Even in the womb of my wife, he loved to move around and kick. He was an active baby. This third son and sixth child entered this world in a different environment. He didn't have to go through a lot of things financially that the other kids had to go through. The other kids had to grow up really fast because this was another child that was coming into our family that needed to be loved.

We had always dreamt about having a big family but no one had ever told us about the finances we would need support a big family. I have never seen a family of our size living on the streets. I believe God really takes care of big families. I was like father Abraham because everywhere we went it was like a whole tribe was following us. A lot of people laughed and mocked us and some even called us stupid for having that many children but I am *so glad* that the Lord *never* allowed our enemies to laugh and mock us to shame because he always had a ram in the bush in every trial that we went through. The Lord even allowed us to help some of those people that had laughed at us. Sometimes I think the Lord was using us to minister to people about him even when we didn't say one word. The children themselves were just a testimony of the wonders and the grace of God and continue to be so.

Our church declared that "every member has a ministry and every ministry has a Pastor", so I spoke to my Pastors about the ministry the Lord put inside of me in Japan and they blessed it. My wife and I started a faith-based Outreach Ministry called Christlike Flavor Ministries, a ministry that was covered by our local church. Christlike Flavor was a blessing because it consisted of people from other churches and my Pastors allowed us to use the facilities at the church to conduct our meetings and opened up the church for us to do programs and events as long as we were winning souls for Jesus.

The year of 2002 was a wonderful year; I saw the vision come to pass that the Lord was showing me in Okinawa, Japan. When we started Christlike Flavor Ministries I had asked a couple of other people to help me get the ministry off of the ground. I explained the vision of the ministry and what God was calling me to do in our city. When I first came to them and told them what the Lord was going to do, one of them thought that wasn't a good idea because Gospel Hip Hop at that time wasn't popular and all they thought we should do was preach on the streets. That would have been nice, but God gave me strategic things that he wanted me to do and how to bring people to him. One young man came along to partner with us because we needed help with administrative things and he wasn't quite sure what God was doing in his life but he said he could find it through helping me. Once I got both of them on the same page about what I needed done to make this ministry run smooth we begin to see the Lord open doors and do things in our lives that we had never seen done.

The Lord began to send rappers, singers, dancers and comedians and people with all kinds of spiritual and natural gifts. There were all types of testimonies of adults and teenagers coming off the streets, giving their lives to Jesus and throwing away the drugs and alcohol. The ministry consisted of rappers, singers, dancers, and Gospel DJ"s, comedians, actors, ministers and spoken Word poets. We were going out into the streets feeding people and gathering the souls in the streets bringing them into the house of the Lord.

There were just miracles and blessings that were following everything that we did. I saw people that were once on the streets get cleaned up and use their gifts to bless the Lord and others. We were going to churches and being a blessing to their ministries and going on the streets wining souls for Jesus. I was so happy because the Lord was working everything out for us; it was like we were the talk of the city. Once the word got out about the ministry and what we were doing, the ministry became popular overnight and everyone that had a calling or gifts began to come and want to partner with what we were doing. It was like going out on the streets and winning souls was the popular thing to do. Young and old began to see the importance of snatching people up out of the pit of hell and restoring lives and living for Jesus.

I was told that the older people in churches weren't into rap and dance and that they didn't want to see their youth get involved in such a thing. What some people didn't realize was that the devil was a minister of music and whether they knew it or not, he was already influencing their youth with ungodly music. The Bible says in Isaiah that he was covered with every precious stone. The devil, who was called Lucifer at that time, was very cunning and sneaky and when God cast him out of heaven he was stripped of everything except his cunning ability to deceive. If someone fires you, they will take your position away but they can never take your knowledge of the things that you learned about that job. Satan is using music in this hour to lure our young people into violence, pre-marital sex, and other ungodly things that displease the Lord Jesus Christ. According to research, music is the only thing that can enter your mind, and remain without your permission. This is why you can remember a jingle or song from twenty years ago like you heard it yesterday.

The Lord showed me that you have a minister that is involved in every ministry such as battered wives, food pantry, evangelistic teams, drug and alcohol, net cares and care groups but you rarely have anyone that goes out to stand up and minister to those that are involved in the Entertainment industry, to those who are responsible for influencing the minds of our children through various media. The Lord showed me in a vision that this is what he wanted me to get involved with and see people come to know him in a delightful way.

Full Time Ministry

I had always dreamt of working full time for the Lord one way or another. I remember preaching as a child and seeing children set free and delivered. I had a brief encounter of going full time when I wasn't working, believing that football was going to take my family and I to the next level financially. The difference was, I wasn't making any money, but I was spending a lot of time with God.

I used to wake up at six in the morning and go outside on my patio and call upon the Lord, and it seemed as if the wind would start blowing and I felt such a peace come over me. The Lord would give me such spiritual revelations about Scriptures and people that were in the Bible that at first it was scary. The Lord had given me a word about not leaving your post. I began to dig into his Word and preach to myself about not being afraid and fighting for what I believed in.

My pastor would always come up to me and let me know that he was proud of me and that he wanted me to pray about the finances of the church so that he could bring me on full time. I always knew that the Lord would work that out in his own timing so I always let my Pastor know that I was going to pray but as soon as the Lord was ready for me to go full time he was going to do it, because I wanted to be a blessing to my church and my leaders. The Lord gave me a word concerning "Suddenly" and He began to tell me that I was going to suddenly be promoted so I began to thank Him for His grace and mercy.

I was coming to church and coming to everything that was going on at the church plus I was working overtime to take care of my family and I was dedicated to the outreach ministry the Lord had put in my spirit. It began to get a little tiresome though, because I had so many things on my plate, but I remained faithful to God and my church. There were plenty of days I would get up and be in meetings all morning and then go to work from noon to nine at night and then I would be at other meetings or functions at night and I served faithfully in that capacity for about two years.

My body was broken and bruised and I wouldn't have it any other way because Jesus done it all for me. I remember telling people on my job that once I got finished evangelizing to everyone there that the Lord was going to move me into full time ministry. I was faithful in the little things, I was faithful in natural things first and then the Lord blessed me with the spiritual blessings He had in store for me.

That is where we mess up as Born-again Believers: We always think spiritual and there is nothing wrong with that, but our homes and lives and families are being destroyed because the devil has us so wrapped up in the spiritual world that we become blind to the earthly assignments our spirit man is being equipped for.

I remember Friday afternoon being rushed with calls all day at work and then getting up and working that Saturday morning and then going to an outreach right after that and I can still hear the supervisor say, "Monday is going to be a beast." Mondays were always terrible far as the phone calls; we would have phone calls come in from all over the world and you had to make sure that every customer felt as if though they were the only person in the world that had a problem. I see now why I was getting this training. God was getting me ready to really love and encourage his people. In ministry, you have good days when everything goes well and then you have those days when it seems like the roof is going to cave in on you; the Lord had been preparing me from day one.

One Sunday morning everything seemed to be going well; I was just happy to be living and knowing that the Lord had blessed my family and I to live another day. What I didn't know was that my "Suddenly" was here. Everything that I had dreamed about and hoped for was knocking at my door. I remember coming to church and praising God and just listening to the things my Pastor was saying and applying them to my life. After church, I was doing the same typical thing and that was praying for people and listening to their praise reports as well as their prayer requests. When I left out of the church, my Pastor started talking with me about various matters and then he said those Godly words that I had been waiting for my whole life, "Are you ready to join us here at the church full time?" *Was I ready? Of course!* I said yes and he encouraged me to do things decently and in order, to give my employer two weeks notice. I was so happy; I remember that day as if it were yesterday. I just kept saying, "Lord, you are real and every praise that I have within me is Yours forever for Your mercy and Your grace." I recalled all of the hard times I went through in my life and it was like every problem that I had was being cast or tossed into a giant lake. My ex-wife that had been with me and kids that had been with me from the beginning were happy because they knew that I had learned a lot through everything and that things could only get better from now on. On top of all of the great news, we had just moved into our second home and my wife shared with me that we had another… surprise! Yes, it was baby number seven, and I couldn't even get upset, this one was on me (smile).

This seventh child's name spoke of God putting us in an appointed placed in our lives. When he was born we called him Mini Me. He looks like a replica of me. He had my personality and everything. If I had tried to deny him, the judge would have put me *under* the jail house. He had a strong and cocky build but yet he was so handsome and cute. His hair was very wavy and shiny silky black. His eyes were a gorgeous and brown. As I looked over at him in that bed I knew that God had blessed me with him. He was born on April fool's Day, so maybe that had something to do with his playfulness. His hands and feet were very wide and he was shaped like a running back and even now when he plays with his other brothers he is like the shining bud.

We called him Bam-Bam, because he was that thick and heavy handed. It didn't take him long to get tangled up with another person if they were trying to take advantage of him. While I am writing this part about my seventh child, my face is lighting up. I love all my kids but there is something about him that makes me smile and light up. I think he will be the one that goes on to college to play professional football. I call him my Ruff Dude because he doesn't care *who* you are, he will fight you like you aren't anything. I am really trying to work with him on that now because he has a little temper on him and I am teaching him the pros and cons to life. The only thing I would say is that I pray that the Lord calms him down before he gets older. As his father, I declare that he shall take that strength and channel it into powerful things for God.

Change

I had just finished writing one of the very first books the Lord had placed in my spirit called the *Making of a Madman*. This was a book about my life, and I thought my book was done. We had just had our eighth and final child which I call my baby, baby, baby, who I will always love. I named her after a famous actress. She came out so dark chocolate and creamy but she looked just like me and of course her mother, thank God. I loved her like no other, I guess with every child it makes you happy to see what you help create or what God allowed you to create just to see their sweet face. I love all my children but I also love what each one of them displays about God, about us, and about their unique personality.

I remember she was born on the day we had a major hurricane and I remember fighting my way back through traffic to see her little face. I felt a sadness because I knew that I was done having children. My wife had started singing and starting her career and I knew that we had to take a break from the baby making abilities that we both had. My baby girl was a mean baby; she didn't want anyone to be in her face, including me. I would love to kiss her and brush my face against hers but because she had dry skin I guess it would irritate her like crazy and she would grab my face and just try to take my beard off. One day my baby and I really bonded and she allowed me to brush my face on hers; it was so funny that we had to video record it and until this day we have a very strong bond.

I thought everything was going pretty good. I had just gotten a vasectomy so that we could not have any more children so that we could enjoy life and the children that God blessed us with. What I didn't know was that my life was about to take a dramatic shift and change. My wife was frustrated that she hadn't gotten a recording deal. It was her desire to sing on a national level and I supported that dream. She went to London to sing at a conference and when she returned to America she never acted the same. My wife signed with a management company out of Atlanta without letting me know because she had lost faith in my ability to manage her. I would try to encourage her but she began to question God's will and His plan for her life. Every time I would ask her had she read her Bible or had she been spending time with God, she would lash out at me. I tried to pray with her and show my love to her but she kept resisting me. I would buy all types of ministering tapes and give them to her but she wouldn't accept them. She started blaming the church that we were attending on the time we weren't spending together. The same outreach that we had labored over lacked interest for her. She stopped showing interest in it altogether so I began to work on my own in the ministry.

I had a conversation with my Pastors about it and they even offered a place on staff for a couple of hours a day just two days a week which she did for a while but quit. She started saying things like, "You are going to make it, but when you do, I won't be with you." She didn't want anything to do with God or His love. We were well known in our city and a lot of people looked up to us in a lot of areas around town and in the Christian arena.

I was promoted to Assistant pastor at my church and I was looked at by all of my peers as a blessing. I couldn't believe what was happening and I began to pray with everything in me that she would stop listening to the devil and love the Lord once more. I was teaching and preaching the Word of God and she had stopped supporting me because she was mad that the management company couldn't get her a singing deal. What was I to do? I was going crazy because I didn't think nor could I believe that she would continue to allow the devil to deceive her about who God was and what He really meant to her, but just as the devil had lied to one third of the angels he lied had to her; it seemed like she was buying into the lies.

One Thursday night, my wife said she was going to one of her dance group rehearsals. We both managed several groups in our city so I never thought anything of it. I was actually happy because I felt like she had shaken the devil off, and was renewing her relationship with God. It was about six in the evening when she left, she said she would be home around nine that night.   When nine-thirty rolled around, I called her to make sure she was okay, but there was no response. I called again a little later and still there was no answer so I figured she was talking and left her cell phone in the car. The next time I looked up it was midnight. She called to tell me that she went to some friend's house to celebrate after the dance rehearsal, but the music playing in the background didn't sound godly. She wouldn't allow me to ask her any questions and she hung up. I fell asleep.

My wife came in the next day, around three in the morning and she just didn't look the same. Something about her spirit seemed wrong and she wouldn't look at me. She slept on the other side of the bed and she hadn't done that since our time in Japan. I figured that she was just having another one of her moments. From that day forward, it set a tone in our house. She didn't want to discuss anything with me nor did she want to go back to church. We were in the process of getting our new home built and it was beautiful six bedroom, five bath home with three stoves with a brick driveway. God had just poured his blessings out on us and things on the outside were going very well, but inside, a change was going on.

Mother's Day Sunday was the last day that I ever saw my wife as I once knew her. We got up and went to church but she didn't want to ride with me. I had a lot of things to do around the church but that was normal. All of the Pastors and their wives were asked to sit on stage, but my wife wouldn't come. It was embarrassing and humiliating because everyone there looked up to us. My mom and dad tried talking to my wife about sitting with me on stage, to not strike the rock like Moses did. When the service was over, we were supposed to go out to dinner but she didn't follow me; she went straight home with the kids.

I thought she was behind me but she turned off and went home and she wouldn't answer her cell phone. When they got home, she told the children that she was going to the store to get some bread and she would be right back. She told the children not to answer the phone, so when I called I didn't get an answer. I called around everywhere looking for her and the children but no one had seen her. I went back to service that night because I had to minister but I got a call from the children saying that their mother hadn't been home and they were hungry.

I immediately called my mother in law and got one of the other ministers at the church to minister for me and went home. When I got home, my children were scared and our dog was exhausted from being caught in the screen door all of that time. I tried calling my wife wondering what was going on and she finally answered saying that she was *never* coming home again and hung up.

I panicked and started praying and calling our friends that my wife might have contacted and maybe tried to reach out to for help. No one had heard anything but everyone kept saying that they had noticed a difference in my wife when she got to church. Some said that my wife had said a couple of times to them that she wanted to give up. I had to call my Pastors the next morning because I was supposed to be at work and I couldn't be there because I had no one there to help watch the kids.

I was so ashamed and humiliated because I had just been prophesied to by one of the largest televangelists in the world about God increasing my territory. I couldn't understand what was going on and didn't know why it was going down like this. Every thought you can imagine came upon me. We had eight beautiful children, a beautiful home, money in the bank, living our dream life; we were one of the up and coming young couples in our city that was destined to do great things for God and we were nearly debt free. I just couldn't understand what I had done to deserve this; I had even given up football for the third time to be with her and keep my family intact. I loved my children and my wife; I just didn't get it.

My wife came home the evening of the next day looking disheveled. She didn't want to speak to the children or me. She didn't look the same and she was using profanity; it appeared as though another spirit was in control. I asked her had she been out with a man and she finally told me yes. She told me she had been out of town and that she was with a man that she had been involved with while we were in Japan. My heart sank. For any man that has ever been told that your wife has been cheating on you, it just does something to your manhood.

I had always lifted my wife up and tried to give her the best of everything. I worshipped the very ground that she walked on and she couldn't do any wrong in my eyes. I forsook football, my friends, and even my family at times just to make her happy. I had given this woman eight children that I will *never* regret. I could have left her like a lot of men that had left their Baby Mommas in high school, but I didn't; I stayed right there and stuck it out like a man.

She said that she had fallen out of love with me and that she loved him, this man whose eyes were as blue as the sea, who was fair to look upon, according to her. I was the loving father of eight and a faithful husband to one. Over the years, I thought I had proven that.

My family had come from such a long way; we had traveled the country together. To the outside world, we were the perfect couple. I had never made it my agenda to tell anyone what had happened in our past. Besides, we had been doing great, what would have been the point? We were Assistant pastors, founders of a very successful urban outreach program and great parents. I never thought twice about my wife's late night dance rehearsals with her background dancers. After all, we were always doing something in the community and she wanted to be the best.

I remember calling her and asking where she was and each time that happened, she'd yell in the phone for me not to question her whereabouts and hang up. The children would call me at the office and say that they were hungry. When I would ask where mom was the kids would tell me they had not seen her all day. Without warning, things took an even more serious turn. My brother who lived a few doors down from my home called in at the office and asked why I had not told him that I was moving. I assured him that I was *not* moving. I quickly panicked when he began to describe the moving truck parked in front of my house loading up furniture. I don't remember even ending the call with him. I drove as fast I could to stop the inevitable; this could not be happening.

That very morning she was so nice to me; it was like we were in high school all over again. She had just apologized for all the things that had happened and promised that things were going to be different between us from now on. I believed her; I had no reason not to but my world came to a complete stand still when I walked through my front doors. My house was so bare that my voice echoed throughout the rooms. Where was my furniture? Where were my children? Where was my wife?

It seemed like hours as mere minutes rolled by. One day while I was in church my cell phone rung and my heart began to race. I didn't recognize the number so I answered. "Daddy, can you come get us?" *My babies!* With the help of her mother who, for years had resented the fact that I had gotten her daughter pregnant some fourteen years prior, I got my children back. I soon learned that her late night dance rehearsals had resulted in her pregnancy from a young lover.

Outraged by the news, I was ready for revenge. I was ready to hurt anyone in my path. My mind was blown away; my wife and I had agreed to my vasectomy so we wouldn't have any more kids and now she was pregnant from another man, the father surprisingly young. I almost lost heart, and even now as I am writing, some of the things that happened to me still bring tears to my eyes.

I was *crushed*; I remember thinking back to all of our accomplishments and thinking: Lord we have ministered to churches and schools, we've ministered at city-wide events, we've done television appearances and interviews, even hosted outreach events, reaching many from preachers to prisoners and we have seen hundreds of people set free and delivered... so why is this happening to us? I cried like a baby because I had prayed with thousands of people seeing the anointing of God set them free, but I couldn't even help my own wife be set free.

I had sat up for hours with certain couples and saw the anointing of God heal their marriages but I couldn't even find anyone that had the anointing to help save my marriage. My mother had always warned me, "Son, never ask a woman a question you really don't want to know the answer to, because she will tell you," and boy I wished I would have listened to her sage advice. The words that wife shared with me that night had made me feel like I was the lowest thing in the earth and that nothing I had ever done for my family meant anything to her, not even me giving up football.

She reminded me of what she had told me several years earlier, that I was going to make it but she wasn't going to be there when I did. I didn't eat for thirteen days, nor did I drink anything. I was praying and fasting and asking God to change her mind but the more I prayed, the worse it got. The more I fasted, the more my wife resisted our marriage covenant. I remembered looking into my children's eyes telling them every time their mother left and we didn't see her again for a couple days, that God was going to change her heart and that she was coming home to stay.

All kinds of thoughts entered my mind about having a research team to get together and find out just where my wife was going when she left, but the Lord didn't allow me to do that. I felt like he was doing a work in me even though it didn't feel good. I knew that the Lord said He wouldn't put more on us than we could bear and I felt I could bear the pressure and that, this too, would pass.

There were people that I had asked to help me reach my wife

but some of them told her that I had disclosed our personal business to them and immediately that drove my wife further from me.   I really felt as though I had no friends. Thoughts of murder and suicide entered my mind but every time I would think about those things, God would minister to me and encourage me to hang on. I had rage and bitterness rise up in me because I thought that certain friends were siding with my wife, saying that she need to be happy and that I was always at church and that is why she left me.

I felt like a lot of my male friends deserted me. I wondered *where are all of the people that I sacrificed my life* for, *who I was there for when they needed my help.* I felt deserted and that my life was coming to an end, none of the prophecies meant anything to me, none of the encouraging words about my life that people spoke years before was there to comfort me in my time of need and none of the people that I had laid down my life down for had stayed with me like Uriah stayed with King David during the war even though King David had him killed.   I was full of hurt and shame and unforgiveness towards my wife and this mystery man she was seeing.

I had to step down as an Assistant pastor at my church to work on repairing my family. This situation brought shame to a lot of people that we knew. I tried to cover my wife and therefore I didn't let the cat out of the bag about her infidelity. My outreach ministry was scattered and the ministry couldn't support itself anymore; rumors about what people thought was going on were being spread like wild fire that couldn't be put out fast enough.

People began to blame me for the deterioration of our marriage. They just couldn't fathom a woman leaving eight children behind and a husband of nearly fifteen years. Some people who were already jealous of me began to talk about me and tried to form their own ungodly relationship with my wife. All along, I was just trying to not strike the rock and allow the devil to take advantage of me during my test of faith. I wouldn't want my worst enemy to go through what I went through. I would continually ask the Lord to allow me to talk with this man, but it never happened.

God, in all of His wisdom was withholding this confrontation. I was still full of rage and strife. God knew I wasn't ready to meet him or talk with him. I would have blown my witness of who Christ really is and what He stood for. The Lord told me during the time I was crying and asking questions that "Son, she left me too and I love her *more* than you can *ever* imagine." He talked to me about Stephen the deacon-evangelist and Jesus the Christ that died for all the sins of the world and how they forgave and didn't want anything to be held to the account of the people that did wrong to them. I was amazed by this revelation and I began to view this whole situation in a different light. I saw that I needed to forgive in order to be set free from the pain, bitterness, and shame I felt.

One day I was in my bedroom and I heard a buzzing sound and I thought it was a bee or some type of bug, but as I looked and listened carefully the sound was coming from up under my bed on my wife's side. It was a cell phone that my wife had that I didn't know about, and it was buzzing because she had forgotten it at home and she was trying to hear her messages. She had developed a pattern of coming home for a couple of days and leaving for a couple of days. When I opened up the phone I was shocked. I saw this young kid's face on the phone. He couldn't have been any older than nineteen or twenty, but this couldn't be.... no way. I found his number in the phone and I called. He answered the phone and was shocked because he thought it was my wife.

I had a minister on the phone that had been praying for my wife as well and I began to speak to him with the love of the Lord. He said he didn't know that my wife had eight children and he didn't even know that she was still married. She had lied to him and had made it appear as though she was from another city with only one child. At the time that I spoke with him, he had just turned twenty and my wife was pregnant by this guy. The pain of that truth was indescribable.

I know people who have gotten locked up for life for killing someone that had an affair with their spouse. The Bible speaks in proverbs about a defrauded man and the vengeance that he seeks. In our society, we call it a crime of passion. Even though every fiber of my being wanted to lash out, the Lord inside of me reminded me of Stephen and Jesus and all of the people that have been killed by angry people, but they (Stephen and Jesus) still chose to forgive. I talked with the young man for a while and just shared the love of Christ with him and prayed for him and I forgave him with all my heart and he knew that. He felt bad about what was happening and attempted to break it off, but my wife didn't want it that way.

One day I came home from work and everything in my house

was gone, including my children. I didn't know where they were or what had occurred; all I knew was that I was standing inside a shell of a home. I felt like the hounds of hell knew that was the last straw that I could take; sin was crouching at the door, waiting for me to make the wrong choice, but I just lifted my hands up and said, "Father, I always said that I would serve you all the days of my life." I remembered the Scripture in Psalms that said God would prepare a table before me in the presence of my enemies. When the devil thought he could eat up my flesh, he stumbled and fell because the Lord was with me right when I needed Him.

My wife, pregnant with another man's child, left me to be with him. Even after my wife left me with nothing and had the baby, I still accepted her back when she and the guy were on bad terms. I had to put forgiveness to the test and when I look back on it now, I know I've been proven and well prepared. I felt like Hosea when he continued to pursue and rescue his wife that was prostituting herself to other men. God wouldn't allow him to leave her because the message God was demonstrating to his prophet was that betrayal was the same way he felt when Israel was prostituting herself with other gods.

Many didn't understand why I made the attempt to take her back. We could get through this, right? But things were never the same between us. She was gone mentally; she did as she pleased, came and went as she pleased, but after fourteen years of it all, I had decided I could not take it anymore and told her to leave. She had been boasting to others, "Maurice isn't going *anywhere.*" *Who could blame her for believing that?* I had stuck it out all these years.

I could not pinpoint the moment boldness sparked within me to finally take a stand, but I filed for divorce. Although she was served with the papers, she had decided she was not going to sign our marriage away. She had decided she wanted it both ways- to have legal ties and benefits to me while living with her new lover.

Familiar with her new lover, I convinced him that it was not her, who had filed for divorce, as he had been told, but in fact I had filed and I needed him to get her to sign the papers. He was now the new father to her ninth child and he had every right to know the truth. He was shocked to learn that he had been tricked and now trapped. The divorce was the easiest experience I had endured the entire fourteen years of our marriage.

To prove her love to him, my wife relinquished all her rights to the house, the assets, and four of our eight children. I kept the house and she returned all the furniture. It was really hard to part with my youngest four, the youngest being only one year old.

My life felt like dominos toppling down when the church asked that I step down because the „situation" didn't reflect well on the ministry. What was a 'situation' for many was my life; suddenly I found myself, a single father of eight with no gainful employment. Not having a job was *not* an option. Not only did I have custody of four of my eight children but I was still responsible for child support for my other four children. I felt like my church family had turned their backs on me when I needed them the most.

I was offered a job by one of the Pastors of my church, a multi-millionaire business owner. He expressed his shock to hear about my situation and knew about all things I had done over the years to bless people. He blessed me to work as a carpenter on a construction site. That was a blessing because that allowed me to bring in money for my children and enabled me to pay my bills. He paid me top dollar; I had found favor in his sight. There were plenty of days I just wanted to die. I had no reason to live, right? I had to work out in the cold and heat when I could have been working from my office praying for people. I found myself upset with God and my ex-wife and her lover but one day on the job, the Lord spoke to me and said, "Son, *I* was a carpenter by trade. I am working this out for your good." That blessed me and kept my spirit encouraged until I was accidentally shot with my nail gun and the nail went into my leg. My boss had to come and take it out with a *hammer*. I must say, most of my messages came from working out there with those six guys and seeing the hand of God move on my life even in this.

I never wanted my children separated from me, becoming and apart of some other man's life; I never imagined being without them. I trusted my ex-wife with every seed that came out of me, to be there for me until death did us part. I thought that we would grow old together and reminisce about the time that we met, that we would tell the world to its face that we made it despite the statistics and man-made laws.

I put all of my trust in her and her dreams. I didn't have the ability to keep her from destroying not only her life but my kids and mine either. When I looked into the faces of my children when they visited, I saw sadness and hopelessness. Their eyes seemed to say, *Dad, how could you let this happen?* Of course they are not old enough to understand everything that happened but I trust the Lord's love for them and that one day he will let them know that I did everything I could to not allow the devil to destroy our family. I will continue to be their father and love them with everything in me.

The law is for the criminals some would say, but I feel like it is a criminal offence to destroy the lives of nine innocent people for self-gratification. I realized through this experience that when a man leaves a woman that has eight children by him for another woman people would really look to kill him but when the roles are reversed, people say, "She needs to be happy." Despite society's lax view, both of them share the same responsibility. There is no male sin and female sin; they both receive the same consequences if they don't repent.

I cried many nights trying to figure out what God's plan was for me. Some nights I didn't hear him talking with me and some nights I did. I was very confused, because I thought at one time that things like this didn't happen to Christian people. I thought only bad people experience stuff like this but not me. *How could this happen to me?* No one had ever really talked about the bad things that happen to good people. I was on fire for the Lord, I had helped people that had needs; I fed the poor, spent time with the lonely, showed up to work and church on time, and as a Believer, had never intentionally tried to hurt or harm anyone else. I had paid my tithes and gave generous offerings for crying out loud! I loved my wife with everything that was in me.

I thought, *how could someone be so evil to someone else especially someone that was in church?* I had spent lots of hours at the church previously before all of these events took place. I was an Assistant pastor for crying out loud! Why weren't these things prevented? *Please, somebody, help me, because I don't see the light,* I would say to myself every day. My Pastor at the time didn't come visit me; some of the same people that I loved, had visited in hospitals, had help to come off of the street and get free from drugs, homosexuality, adultery, and death, didn't show up either. I would ask myself, *where are those people now, when I need them?*

The more I complained, the angrier I became with people about their response to my ordeal and eventually I might have gotten angry with God, but the Lord ministered to me like He ministered to Job. He had my life in his hand; I had been prophesied to before about how God was going to expand my territory and how much love the Lord had for me. I'm telling you this, because it is freeing someone from past hurts.

At this point, I didn't have much of anything; I had to take a sabbatical to take care of my children because my wife was in and out of the house with her new lover. My heart felt like a boulder had been tied to it, my veins felt like they would explode at any minute, leading to my death. I am working as a carpenter, with wood, nails and heavy equipment, no more working for the church in a huge office with the A/C blowing on me in the Florida heat but now I'm outside with my peers.

I think to myself, *they all have problems, I just know that the Lord has not put me out here to witness to them when I am going through so much.* When I realized that I wasn't going anywhere and that the Lord was going to keep me out in the heat and cold until I got over my tribulations, I stopped complaining about them every day and I started to just thank Him for life. Only weeks before, I wanted to whole house to fall on me. He said to me, "Everything that happened to you was for my purpose, so get out there and pastor these guys that really need you, and watch Me take your testimony and make a miracle out of it."

I couldn't do anything but cry. He said, "Son, I was treated far worse and I still had to forgive." So, that's just what I started to do. I truly had to forgive my wife and her lover. I started preaching and seeing guys set free from past hurts. I really came to love my job out in the field. I was one of the top paid guys out there and one of the most respected. I held favor with the owner of the company, a millionaire by hard work who had a testimony of his own. I found out that *his* ex-wife did him the same way but God had blessed him with everything including his children's respect. One day he prophesied to me that I would have even more than he had when it was all said and done. I felt like Joseph in prison, knowing that he had nothing to do with it, but was there none the less. I had to forgive the way Joseph forgave his brothers. I realized that this forgiving thing wasn't going to be easy but if I wanted God to forgive me then I had to forgive my wife and her lover

New Beginnings

My ex-wife and I have divorced and have moved on. Our eight children have been divided, the oldest four with me and the youngest four with her. I wanted all eight of my children because I didn't want them to grow up without being raised in the church and missing out on what they had been used to. I *know* you wanted a text book ending with me winning back my wife and us living happily ever after but just wait one second and continue to read.

I am now happily married to Lisa McClendon, International Recording Artist, and have two more beautiful children through our blended family. I was able to keep my home and my vehicle without going into foreclosure or repossession. My children are happy and my son is starring in a television sitcom in Jacksonville. I have helped to start another evangelism outreach in Jacksonville and I am the part owner of a record label. Lisa and I have moved and I am now the Senior Pastor of The Life Center in Charlotte, NC. God has given me His peace and His love and His wonderful Holy Spirit. God has multiplied everything that I lost and He has given it back to me like He did Job.

I am more respected now than I was then because anyone can hurt or harm someone else but it takes a special person to forgive and forget. The devil tried to change my character towards people but God wouldn't allow it. I hold nothing to their account; neither do I want anything to happen to them. I had gone from sitting in an office in the air condition to building homes in the Florida heat and I no longer hold any grudges about it. There have been many days where I have just cried and thanked the Lord for not allowing me to do something stupid to jeopardize my life or someone else's. It's not worth it.

I know that at this very moment there are people that have to make a choice today, and some day you may have to make the choice as well. Some have walked into rooms with their spouse and caught them in the very act of adultery, and some have found love letters and clothing that have proven to you that someone is in a relationship with your spouse. There are some people that have been approached by others who have seen your spouse with someone else. Some of you have found videos and pictures or even hired people to follow your spouses. The question is when you find out what is happening are you going to forgive? There are people right now who are behind bars or dead wishing they had another chance to rethink the situation. I can't say that I am happy that things turned out this way but I can tell you that I am happy that I am alive and not in jail wishing that I could turn back the hands of time.

Brother, sister, it's not worth it; your life is worth more than this type of drama. I have heard everything from, "You weren't romantic enough to you weren't my type," but one thing that I do know is that someone else's garbage is someone else's treasure. God will put the right person in your life at the right time and that person will stick with you like glue. True love is like Christ- it's always quick to forgive and would love you through anything that comes up. Some people will read this book and think, *I can't do that. I can't forgive someone that slept with my spouse.* I hope you understand you cannot afford to *not* forgive. Your life in eternity depends on it; *nothing* is worth you going to hell over; nothing is worth missing out on the abundance of God's blessings and overflowing miracles.

Forgiveness is so powerful it allowed me to release my ex-wife and the man that she had an affair with. I have talked with him several times since then, and I don't have any animosity towards him and I have truly forgiven him. Life is too expensive to waste it on hating people. I have a work to do and I know that if I don't forgive *both* of them, there's no way that the Lord can forgive me. Someone once said that unforgiveness is like drinking poison and then waiting on the other person to die.

If Stephen in the book of Acts, who was getting stoned, would have never forgiven those who killed him, would Jesus have stood up on the right hand of the Father or would God have killed Paul on his way to Damascus for committing such an evil crime of holding the coats of the men who stoned Stephen? God cannot forgive you if you don't forgive others. No matter how bad I felt getting up night after night, hoping that my ex-wife would come home, it didn't happen. I knew that I had to forgive her and him. Who wants to know their spouse having an affair? The thoughts alone could really mess you up. I had plenty of thoughts of this guy doing all sorts of things with my wife and I felt helpless because I knew that I couldn't hold a grudge or hurt them.

People called me all sorts of names and said that there was no way in Hades they could forgive their spouse for sleeping with someone else, but when I pointed out to them that they could not be forgiven for their own sins, it made them think. Jesus died on the cross so that the worst criminal could be forgiven and have a spot in heaven. I believe that I will reach this dying, hate-filled world with this book and see the prisons empty one day because everyone that was in a situation like I was in will just stop for a moment, breathe…and just forgive.

The Lord answered all of my questions about my life, family, friends, ministry within and my pastors. I just want to say to you that the Lord is real and He has a purpose for your life. You might feel like the world is coming down on you but I know Someone that uses this earth as His footstool, who loves you and sent His son, Jesus to die for your sins. Things *will* get better. Don't give up; you have a purpose in life and the Light, who is Christ, stands confidently at the end of your tribulation. Remember, the trials you face and the things you suffer will work a far more exceeding and eternal weight of glory.

Forgiveness: God's Eternal Plan

Before there was ever a Book of Genesis written, forgiveness caused the world around us to exist. Mankind is the apple of God's eye, always was, and always will be. God's plan to create mankind caused the very movement in heaven to change. Things weren't going to be the same anymore between the Great I Am and Lucifer the Anointed Cherub that covered. I need mankind to understand the position they hold with our Heavenly Father.

When God blessed man, he literally bowed before him in front of creation to let the world know that authority was in man's hand and everything was going to respect him. *Have you ever thought about why God forgave Adam and Eve for what they had done but didn't forgive Lucifer for causing a holy war in heaven?* Before the Lord created the heavens and the earth, spoke light into existence and created mankind, he understood that he had to make a choice to forgive.

The Lord said in Isaiah chapter forty-three verse twenty-five, "I, even I, am he that blotteth out thy transgressions for **mine own sake, and will not remember thy sins**." God knows all things, and a lot of people wonder, *if God knew that Adam and Eve were going to disobey him why did he create them?* Thanks for asking; God gave us all a choice- he didn't create robots; even the angels in heaven had a choice. Even Satan, the head angel at that time, who walked in the very presence of God, that God took his time to create, walked away from God in his own rebelliousness.

True forgiveness is to pardon or excuse a wrong (Matt. 6:12, 14-15), to cancel a debt, to give up claim for revenge or resentment; to re-establish a broken relationship. To forgive is to trust others as if the wrong is forgotten. It includes a new start in attitudes and actions (John 8:11). Just a question: How easy or difficult is it for you to forgive; to be forgiven? Forgiving others opens us up to receive forgiveness from God. Jesus forgave sins (Mark 2:5) and encourages us to forgive each other the same way (Col. 3:13; Matt. 18:22-35). Jesus made it possible for God to forgive us our sins and not just cover them up. Once you ask for forgiveness then you are considered blameless.

God had a plan from the beginning. He knew how much he loved man and he never made a mistake, so when Adam and Eve messed up, he had a plan that would take care of their sin debt. That is why Satan is so upset with you now because he knows that there is nothing that you can do to keep God away from you when you repent. That is why forgiveness is a principle because if you can't forgive others God cannot forgive you and therefore you cannot be fully blessed to access the Kingdom of Heaven.

Shaking the Heavens

God says this about Satan in Ezekiel 28:13-19:

"You **were** the seal of perfection, Full of wisdom and perfect in beauty."

God was proud of what he created; Satan was God's confidante. I picture them talking about everything together, and to a degree, Satan understood God's vision and he was wise enough to relate to the Lord. Unfortunately, he wanted to be God according to Isaiah 14: 13.

Ezekiel 28:13 continues: "You were in Eden, the garden of God; every precious stone **was** your covering: The sardius, topaz, and diamond, beryl, onyx, and jasper, sapphire, turquoise, and emerald with gold."

Satan had the very first Bling-Bling! He was made so every angel could look at him and marvel on his appearance. His vanity would be his downfall.

"The workmanship of your timbrels and pipes was prepared for you on the day you were **created**."

Satan was given such a wonderful talent that music was created in him that when he walked music played and everyone standing around would hear him coming before he got there. He was designed to signal and announce God's presence.

Vs. 14 "You **were** the anointed cherub who covers; I established you; you were on the holy mountain of God; you walked back and forth in the midst of fiery stones.

Satan was God's amour bearer; he knew things about God due to his position and he covered him: he was God's eyes and ears around heaven. Satan walked in the very presence of our Holy Father. Those stones represent the place of prayer. This is why Satan fights intercession. He understood the power of the fiery stones, the sacrifice of praise and prayers.

Vs. 15 "You **were** perfect in your ways from the day you were created, till iniquity was found in you."

Jealousy of mankind, lawlessness, transgression and unrighteousness was found in Lucifer. Iniquity was the secret thoughts that Lucifer held about God and his place in the Kingdom.

Vs. 16 " By the abundance of your **trading You became filled with violence within**, And you sinned; Therefore I cast you as a profane thing **Out of the mountain of God**; And I **destroyed you**, O covering cherub, From the midst of the fiery stones."

Treating the presence of God, the angels of God, and his gifts like merchandise increased his violence within. He wanted to do more than announce the presence of God; he wanted to *be* God. It wasn't enough to be Heaven's commentator.

Vs. 17 "Your heart was **lifted up because of your beauty**; you **corrupted** your wisdom for the sake of **your splendor;** I cast you to the ground, I laid you before kings, that they might gaze at you."

His treasure was outward and it caused him to take his eyes off of his purpose. He wanted to be the *celebrated* cherub, not the covering cherub.   He wanted to be worshipped and he still does. He even proposed that Jesus worship him (Luke 4:1-8).

Vs. 18 "You defiled **your sanctuaries** by the multitude of your iniquities, by the iniquity of your trading; therefore **I brought fire from your midst; it devoured you, and I turned you to ashes upon the earth in the sight of all who saw you.**

Satan corrupted sacred places with his impure motives. Notice that fire came from out of Satan. Hell was never created for humans; it was prepared for Satan and his angels.

Vs. 19, "All who knew you among the peoples are astonished at you; **you have become a horror**, and *shall be* no more forever."

God flipped this beautiful, talented, created angel inside out so he would be exposed for the horror he was. He was the first horror.

Those acts of Satan really angered God. The angel that he created to please and cover him and serve His purpose became jealous because of the plan that God had for man to reign and rule in the earth and not him. I can picture God sharing with Satan his plan for man to rule Eden and showed His soft side to Satan when it came to mankind. Satan thought he could overtake the God of everything, but there was something God didn't let him in on: forgiveness and redemption. The Bible declares that if Satan had known about the plan of salvation, he would have never championed the crucifixion of Christ.

Satan trafficked the other angels and caused them to fall with him. God had to be really heartbroken because he threw Satan and one third of the angels with him out of heaven. That had to really be a horrible day in heaven (it was the first war). God did this because He loved mankind and was going to see His plan through to allow man to rule. When Satan realized there was no more hope for him to ever re-establish that relationship with our Heavenly Father his goal became the destruction of God's relationship with mankind.

When Adam and Eve disobeyed the Lord by eating the fruit on the forbidden tree and listening to the biggest liar that ever existed, that caused a separation to occur between mankind and God. Satan thought that this would cause God to be done with mankind like he was done with him, but God had a plan, and forgiveness became a reality. God had a plan to send his son Jesus to the earth to die for our sins and bring us true redemption. God really loved mankind for him to have put on an earthly suit and die for the sins of the world to bring us back to him with full authority and royalty as if it had never happened.

Forgiveness means to overlook, to release, setting a person free from all hurts, to dismiss, to remit, and suspend a justified penalty. So many people have pressed pause, freezing those who have wronged us at that point of offence and have never truly let it go. Forgiveness is not situational it is truly God; it is an act of love.

Throughout the New Testament, the Bible speaks about forgiveness and love and how they work together. There are people right now that are locked up, in the hospital, in mental wards or just dying inside because they have not truly forgiven that person that hurt them. People are still holding onto unforgiveness with people that have died or moved on. This stops the flow of blessings from overtaking you. Doctors and other experts say that a majority of people that are sick today are people that are holding a lot of hurt and unforgiveness inside of them.

Having unforgiveness only kills the one that holds on to eat or drink it. God cannot bless you if you are not willing to forgive others. Jesus died for the worst criminal that ever walked the planet earth; he forgave the people that drove the nails through his wrists, spit in his face, plucked his beard out, buffed under his eyes and mocked him, gave him vinegar to drink instead of water, scorned and laughed at him when they asked him to prophesy who hit him when his eyes were nearly beaten out. They even gambled over his garments, figuring they were worth more than the Son of the Living God. Jesus said in the book of Mathew that he could have called twelve legions of angels to come down and take care of everything that was happening to him but he understood how important mankind was to the God and he allowed them to do this to him so that scripture might be fulfilled (Psalm 22). He was like a lamb going to the slaughter willfully and one of his last statements was, "Father, forgive them they know not what they do."

In the seventh chapter of the book of Acts, I believe when Stephen saw Jesus standing on the right hand of God as he was being stoned, that Jesus stood up not for the crime, but for the *response* to the crime: it was the act of his forgiveness towards those people and Jesus related to him because he did the same thing on the cross. Stephen asked God not to lay this murder on their charge. How could a man that is being murdered care for the ones that are killing him without cause and still have the love of God in him to be concerned about his killers not being held accountable; Forgiveness.

Forgiveness is an important word. God showed me in a day vision that more people will die and go to hell for unforgiveness than anything else. Small hurts leads to unforgiveness. Get over it and forgive quickly because your blessing is held up until you get it out of your life. Some people think, *I will forgive but I won't forget*. That is a lie straight from hell and the devil uses it to keep God's people chained to unforgiveness. Don't freeze events in your mind of the terrible things people did to you. Whether they are amongst the living or dead please, forgive them, and move on with your life. I know several stories of people that have been sick and as soon as they forgave that person the manifest power of God showed up and healed them. Sometimes we are ignorant to the things of God and it causes us to miss our blessings. Too many people today that are in jail, bad situations, and hell because they chose not forgive. Don't gain a boatload of bitterness and lose your soul in the process. Forgive today.

From My Heart to Yours

To those that thought that it was easy for me to forgive my ex-wife and her lover please read.

This was no ordinary woman to me. I really thought that we were invincible and nothing could ever come between my ex-wife and me. It was like I worshipped the ground that she walked on and my pride was in her. Looking back, I realize that only God alone deserves my worship. I never thought that she would ever betray me or lose her love towards me. I had sacrificed a lot of things to be with her, I had gave up the sport that I loved for many years for her including not going to college the first time around to show her how much I loved her.

I had covered her in so many ways. I had three homes built for her and had eight beautiful children with her. I started an outreach ministry to cater to her singing abilities so she would be able to shine among the best singers in the world. I sacrificed my teenage years running after her and trying to do everything in my power to see her happy. Everywhere we went people would stare and say that we were blessed and that our children were so well behaved.

I had friends in high school who begged me not to ruin my life by marrying her, so I developed an „us against the world" mentality. There was *nothing* on earth that I wouldn't do for her. We had literally been around the world together. I knew her before she even went through puberty. I had risked being shot by her stepfather or put in jail by my attempts to see her. I had covered her in so many ways that you could not even imagine. I knew that one day if we continued to have children together that she could leave me and I would have to pay child support out of my butt. I didn't let anything stop me from loving her. I had turned down so many opportunities to be with people that really had things going on in their lives but I decided to stick with her.

Time and time again I would wonder why I was so into her like that, I never wanted my life to be surrounded by her every move. I could not shake it; I guess I was really in love because I could see no wrong in her. When people warned me about her character flaws, I didn't get mad at her I got mad at them. I was, for lack of a better word, sprung" and it was crazy because I knew in my heart that I was doing the wrong thing for the right reasons. I even brought my whole paycheck home to her and asked if I could have a little spending money; I didn't even know how to write checks.

I never checked on her at first because I trusted her with everything that I had in me. I would give my life to see her happy. I went against my whole family to see her smile. I was not wise about a lot of things during that time of my life. We had something that those around us wanted and that was chemistry and love. I really thought that she was the one for me because even though I saw the signs, I didn't want to listen. At times, I worked two jobs just so we could make it. She never had to work much for anything; I always wanted to make sure that she had the best.

People would always give us compliments and everywhere we went they would prophesy to us about how God was going to bless us and keep us and how we were going to be millionaires and so forth. I really thought that I was out of that divorce zone but I forgot about her curiosity and dissatisfaction with her unfulfilled goals. Her mind was always going even when we slept she would be up sometimes just thinking about things. Her cunning put our marriage at stake.

I made plenty of mistakes now that I look back on our relationship and I see certain things that I could have done better to reach out to her. I'm sure in her mind that she could justify her actions but in the end, because I was the man of the house, I believe the blame was with me. I allowed the strongman to come in and take my family. This is a hard pill to swallow, but God made me the priest of my home and covering for my ex-wife. Because of my business in ministry and focusing more on the lives of others rather than my family, I neglected a part of her that needed my attention. I am man enough to own up to my mistakes and pray that it will help save another marriage.

Nobody wants another man's hands on his prize and that is the way I felt about my wife. We were both innocents when we met and came together. How awesome can that be for one's life? When a man finds a wife he finds a good thing and obtains favor from the Lord and that's what life was like when I was with her. Though we are no longer married, I have re-married because though divorce happens, and it is not God's perfect plan, it doesn't negate the fact that marriage is God-ordained and God honored. I am now in a mutually loving relationship and experiencing the joys of marriage as God intended. Not only did I find favor with God, I found it with people in my community, church, and family. I have shared all of this so you can understand why I am not dead, in jail, or in hell right now. This is my testimony and my life bares witness of it to the glory of God.

Confessions

In the book of Matthew, the 18th chapter and the 21st verse it says, "Then came Peter to him, and said, Lord, how oft shall my brother sin against me, and I *forgive* him? Till seven times? And Jesus said unto him, I say not unto thee, until seven times: but, until seventy times seven."

In this passage of Scripture, God was not giving the disciples any room to hold unforgiveness in their hearts. Sometimes it's hard to forgive someone for hurting you but if you don't forgive them, neither can God forgive you. The Lord spoke to me once and said that there are more people that will not make it into heaven because of unforgiveness than anything else. It wasn't the sins that you would call big that kept a lot of people out of heaven it was not forgiving someone and dying that way. When you forgive someone, it allows God to bless you because he did the same thing for you. If someone has hurt you, give it to the Lord and remember it isn't that person, it is a demonic spirit or influence that is causing them to act that way. You have to pray for them that despitefully use you and say all manner of evil against you falsely for God's sake (Matthew 5).

If you are ready to forgive, repeat the prayer below:

Heavenly Father,

I release (state the person's name) from the sin of (state the issue). Though it caused me pain, I let it go. I forgive them and I give it over completely to you. I ask that you free me from unforgiveness and every sickness and infirmity associated with it. I believe that as I forgive, you forgive me through the blood of Jesus Christ. I receive Him as my Lord and Savior. I ask Jesus to come into my heart and live there. I believe that he died for all sin, including mine. Amen.

If you have repeated this prayer and experienced the power of forgiveness, the author would love to hear from you. Continue to walk in forgiveness by joining your local church and serve God to the best of your ability. Remember, keep on forgiving!

W●RLDwide.

Upcoming Literary Titles

Forgiveness: A New Prescription -The Real Health Plan
Maurice Brailsford

Pops Told Us So
Maurice Brailsford

The Making of a Madman
Maurice Brailsford & Apostle Clifford Kelly, Jr.

One Night Stand
Lisa McClendon-Brailsford

What Do You Do When Loving Him Is Killing You?
Goldia Felder

For Inquiries:
blusoulworldwide@gmail.com

www.ingramcontent.com/pod-product-compliance
Lightning Source LLC
Chambersburg PA
CBHW060157070426
42447CB00033B/2199